BILINGUAL
IN
NATURE

By Adelaide Olguin

Edited by Elissa Mleiel

published with love by

TALKBOX.MOM, inc.

OPENING CREDITS

Thank you to the incredible women who ensured you'll talk like they do with their families in their native language and not like you walked out of a dusty old textbook. (We're especially looking at you, French.)

SPANISH
Aida F. Olguin
Cynthia Ware
Valerie Dominguez
Adriana Villalba
Nadia Ojeda

FRENCH
Joanne Rouzic de Souza
Valérie Renard
Elissa Mleiel
Armelle Bevilis
Justine Cabrero

GERMAN
Sandra Junker
Nadine Burke
Annika Sommer
Janine Unfug
Hanna Anderson
Katherine Williams Olsen

ITALIAN
Emanuela Ciriotti
Liviana Cicconetti
Caterina Piag

CHINESE
Wei Shi
Sunli Rexwinkle
Candy Zuo

JAPANESE
Yumiko Koganezawa
Yuko Wylie
Sachi Nasu
Hiromi Kawaragi

KOREAN
Eunice Ahn
Christine Huh
Jiwon Song
Jisoo Park
Jihyun Hong

HEBREW
Patrizia Hula
Maayan Inger
Ingrid Sherman

PORTUGUESE
Rebeca Lemos
Juliana Reimer
Viviane Castro

RUSSIAN
Daria Andrenko
Yuliia Holomedova
Olga Gorval
Elnara Salimova

When you purchase from TalkBox.Mom,
you're supporting women all over the world.

TABLE OF CONTENTS

There is native speaker audio for every single phrase in this book, plus a system to help you track your progress as you listen, practice, and use your phrases in the **TalkBox.Mom Companion App.**

At the time of your purchase, you received non-transferable app access directly tied to your email address. If you don't already have access to the audio from the time of your purchase, please email your receipt to support@talkbox.mom, so we can get you setup in the app.

To download the TalkBox.Mom Companion App on your phone, search for "TalkBox.Mom Companion App" inside your phone's app store (Android or Apple). After downloading the app, login with your username and password. You can reset your password using your email address on the login page if you have no idea what your password is. We got you!

If you have any other problems or questions, please email support. Our team would love to help you!

◆ **support@talkbox.mom**

HELLO! OF COURSE.

Many people think that learning a language starts with colors, numbers, and the ABC's. But that's what our kids do in preschool after they can already speak the language.

This is not where language learning begins. And starting with the ABC's and colors is definitely not language immersion or the path to fluency.

 There is hardly another civilised nation so dull in acquiring foreign tongues as we English of the present time; but, probably, **the fault lies rather in the way we set about the study** than in any natural incapacity for languages." - *Charlotte Mason*[1]

Learning to use a language looks like starting your day off, greeting each other, and eating in that language. It looks like grocery shopping in that language while helping each other or sometimes hearing kids complain. If your extended family speaks that language, it looks like using that language at family events. If your family doesn't, it looks like telling your child to go back, flush the toilet, and wash their hands in your "secret language." ;) Everyone else will be impressed by your language skills—not knowing how gross your child is being.

At TalkBox.Mom, we help families, like yours, start talking in a foreign language the same exact day you start. You don't wait to talk until year two or year... well, never. You talk from day one.

We can help your family start talking right away because we copy the approach of the best language teachers in the world: parents.

Yes, parents. Think about it. Who taught your kids to talk before they ever learned grammar and reading? You did.

As moms and dads, we teach babies and toddlers all over the world to talk at a native level—the most coveted level of learning a language. We have a higher success rate of teaching languages than high schools, colleges, and universities.

With TalkBox.Mom, we give you the tools to learn and teach another language using our proven roadmap and various fluency approaches based on natural language progression. We also help you lean into the skills you already have to teach a language successfully as a parent.

Plus, everything in our language programs is made by native-speaking women that want you to sound like you're from their country—not like you walked out of an outdated textbook.

And, yes, there is audio for every single phrase in our program. We mean it when we say that we'll give you all the tools to make learning another language feel easy, fun, doable, and the biggest confidence boost you've ever gotten.

And now, with your family, you get to try using a language with this guide and hear it for yourself! So let's get started!

HOW TO GUIDE

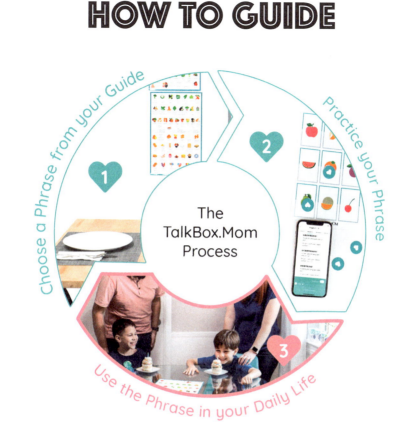

Choose a Phrase from your Guide

Practice your Phrase

1

2

3

The TalkBox.Mom Process

Use the Phrase in your Daily Life

The TalkBox.Mom Process has three completely doable steps to get your family talking!

First, you pick your 1-5 focus phrases. Yes, full phrases—not individual words or verb conjugations.

> But one verb is nothing; you want the child to learn French..." - *Charlotte Mason*[2]

Second, you'll practice the phrases. It's very important to practice your phrases so your children are ready to use them in real life, which brings us to our next step!

Third, you'll use those phrases in real life. The goal is to add the phrases to your outdoor adventures!

By following the TalkBox.Mom Process, you'll be learning to use full sentences with your family and continue to use those phrases in your life.

 Of course, his teacher, will take care... that as he learns new words, they are *put into sentences and kept in use from day to day*." - *Charlotte Mason*[3]

Here's a closer look at how these steps will look in your day with your family as well as some things to avoid!

Step 1: Pick 1-5 Focus Phrases

🕐 Time Needed: typically 30 seconds to 2 minutes

The first step is to choose only one to five focus phrases. This step is actually really hard for many people because it's so tempting to want to start with, well, everything! However, I promise that you'll learn everything much faster if you focus on one to five phrases.

Why? By focusing on a small number of phrases, you'll learn those phrases faster and deeper than if you spread yourself too thin. You'll also be able to give the phrases the attention they need to be practiced and used in real life. It's much more doable to implement two phrases with your child than 20 in a single day.

 That they should learn a few—two or three, four or five—new French words daily...." - *Charlotte Mason*[4]

Even if it feels "too light" for you as the parent, the goal isn't that you're learning a whole bunch of things. It's that you're using the language. Using the language requires a deep and narrow focus that consistently grows.

This small focus helps lay a strong foundation. As these phrases are really internalized when they are practiced and used, they start to feel like second nature (aka a second language). When this happens, the following sets of phrases you work on continue to become even easier, especially if you start your first box in the TalkBox.Mom program because it's designed to help you make exponential progress.

So please allow yourself to learn everything faster by focusing on one to five phrases—not by focusing on everything all at once.

To start, have your child color in the hearts of one to five phrases in this guide.

I recommend starting with just one to two phrases your first day so you can take those two phrases through the entire TalkBox.Mom process.

You can choose the phrases in front of your child, you can give your child two good options and allow them to choose the one that they're more excited about today, or you can let your child choose.

Have you or your child heart these phrases in the TalkBox.Mom Companion App for easy access to the audio and progress tracking.

Open your TalkBox.Mom Companion App included with your purchase or verified gifting of this book (see page 4 for instructions). Click on the book icon 📘 on the home screen. Then select Bilingual in Nature and the language that you're using. After selecting your language, the top slides to different sections that match the bolded words in this guide.

Next, have you or your child click the heart 💜 next to the chosen phrases. Now your phrases will easily be accessed from the home screen under "Learning." This will help save you time in the next steps!

For families with multiple children, you can switch off children hearting phrases or have your other children help in the following steps. If your child does not look at screens, they can listen to the audio without viewing your phone.

Step 2: Practice your Phrases

🕐 Time Needed: 2 minutes to 10 minutes

Note: The more phrases you've chosen, the longer this step will take.

For older children with required foreign language time of 30, 45, or 60 minutes a day, this step can expand to that time requirement, keeping in mind that Step 3 will give you additional time, especially as you're able to use more of the language.

The second step is to practice your chosen phrases. There are three main ways to practice your phrases, and they're listed here in order of importance: (1) practice with the native speaker audio, (2) practice in situations, and (3) practice with emotions.

1 Practicing with the Native Speaker Audio

That children should learn French orally, by listening to and repeating French words and phrases."
- *Charlotte Mason*[5]

You might be tempted to skip this step if you, as the parent, can pronounce the phrases or if you're a native speaker, but don't skip it! It's important to have that extra input that's not just you. Get that extra input! There's a noticeable difference if you skip practicing with the native speaker audio.

To practice with the native speaker audio, navigate to your learning section or the book in the TalkBox.Mom Companion App as described in the previous step. Be sure "autoplay" is turned off in the app because you want to practice one phrase at a time—not repeat all your phrases together.

Have you or your child announce what the phrase is in English and tell everyone to repeat after the native speaker. For example, "We're going to hear how to say [phrase] in [language name]. Have fun repeating after each word. If you can, say the full phrase after her at the end."

The native speaker will say the phrase word by word (or tone by tone for Chinese) while pausing for your family to repeat. Then she will say the full phrase and pause for your family to repeat.

If the full phrase feels like too much at first, that's fine! Just say the phrase word by word. After a couple of days, you'll feel ready to say the entire phrase.

After you finish repeating the phrase, have you or your child ask everyone what the phrase means. If some family members aren't sure, remind your family what it means, practice with the audio again, and ask again what the phrase means until everyone is on the same page.

When your family repeats with the audio, celebrate that everyone tried! Refrain from correcting anyone's pronunciation or being hard on yourself for how you sound. Why?

For family members over fours years old, it can take a couple of weeks to a couple of months to hear the sounds in the new language, and when you can't hear the sounds, you can't fix the sounds. So if you tell someone they're saying it wrong, and they can't hear it and fix it, they'll just be annoyed with you.

But you can start hearing better as you're having fun as you listen and practice with the native speaker audio. The keyword here is fun! Stressed out people have trouble hearing better. So be sure not to stress your kids or yourself out by focusing on sounding perfect.

Focus on having fun so you can continue to hear the sounds over time and improve as you continue to practice and use your phrases.

2 Practice the Phrase in Situations

Once your family repeats with the native speaker audio, practice that same phrase in a situation rather than moving on to the next phrase. You can absolutely play the audio again and again as you practice the phrase together.

To make this phrase real for your family and make your practice age-appropriate, decide together when you could add this phrase to your life. You can either set up that specific situation and practice using the phrase in that situation, use the phrase as you pretend you're in that situation, or say the phrase like you're in that situation. Yes, details immediately below.

For example, if the phrase is, "Follow the path," you could walk over to a path with your family and have one family member say the phrase and another family member follow the path. Then switch until everyone has had a turn!

Or you could pretend there is a path in your living room and have one family member say the phrase and another family member follow the path. Then switch until everyone has had a turn!

Or you could sit on the couch or ground outside (because it's just one of those days) and have a family member say the phrase like they see a path and want someone to follow it.

You can raise the stakes in any of these situations and say, "Say, 'Follow the path,' like you're on a secret mission in the jungle." Or, "Say, 'Follow the path,' like it leads to ice cream!" We call this game,

"Say It Like." Let the creativity spill over here. Younger and older kids will have different ideas that match what's fun and interesting for their age level.

3 Practice your Phrase with Emotions

Here's where you can have even more fun! This is an extra important step if you've ever corrected your child's pronunciation, making them shut down or be less willing to try. And it's equally important if this has ever happened to you, and you have hesitations about speaking another language. Remember, it's more important to have fun than to sound perfect.

To practice with emotions, we have three outlets. The first is choosing raw emotions and having someone say a phrase with that emotion.

For example, "Say the phrase, 'Follow the path," like you're really happy!"

You can choose any emotion or state, like excited, sleepy, scared, nervous, creepy, or hangry.

The second way to practice emotions is by saying the phrase like you're someone else. Choose a person your child knows. This could be a friend, superhero, or character.

For example, "Say the phrase, 'Follow the path," like Grandma."

The third way to practice a phrase with emotions is with music! Different styles of music can make you feel different ways. You could sing your phrase like an opera singer or rap artist. Whatever musical style you or your child likes or wants to try. And you don't have to be on tune to make this jam session effective.

After you practice your phrase, go back to Step 1 and listen to your next phrase repeating these two steps.

Q: What should I do if my child is an infant or toddler?

A: Practice and use your phrases around your infant or toddler! He or she doesn't need to repeat with the audio or practice saying the phrases yet to learn. This is a great age for them to take in what you're doing and learn from you.

Step 3: Use your Phrases

At this point, "lesson time" is over, and real life begins!

It only be a little lesson, ten minutes long, and the slight break and the effort of attention will give the greater zest to the pleasure and leisure to follow."
- *Charlotte Mason*[6]

Now it's time to encourage everyone to try to add your phrases to your day as many times as you can while you're having fun outside!

Celebrate any attempt at using phrases. Even if only a word or two come out!

If you forget to use a phrase and remember it moments later, use it right then! Start building that habit.

And please! Don't deprive yourself of looking at the phrase or listening to the audio again to help you say that phrase. You might feel like you're cheating or like you need to force yourself to remember. Nope. Make it very easy for yourself until it feels like second nature. If it doesn't feel like second nature, you need to look and listen again to continue to build that neural pathway.

Now, if someone in your family uses one of your phrases and another family member forgets what the phrase means, tell them what it means! You want to make it easy for your children to know what's going on. They just put in all the work to learn their first language, which now feels super easy to them. If the second language feels difficult, there can be more resistance.

So say the phrase in English if someone is confused and then again in the language that you're learning. We call this the "Ice Cream Sandwich" because you first say the phrase in the other language, then in English to clarify, and then in the other language again.

Your Daily Schedule

 The daily French lesson is one that should not be omitted." - *Charlotte Mason*[7]

The following day, you can continue with the same 1-5 phrases if you don't feel comfortable yet adding those phrases to your life. You'll repeat the first and second steps of the TalkBox.Mom Process, and if you can, use the phrases that day to complete the third step.

Keep in mind that it's not always possible to complete all three steps, so please celebrate what you are able to do—instead of focusing on the little things you missed. It's not so much what you do in one day, but what you do over several days, weeks, months, and years.

If one or more of your phrases feel comfortable to your family, you can take those phrases out of your focus list and replace them with new phrases. You'll continue to use the removed phrase but don't need to practice them daily.

To mark a phrase that your family is using in real life, check ✔ the phrase in your book and in the app. Remember, it's not that your family "knows" the phrase. It's that you're using it.

This means that if you still need to peek sometimes at the phrase on your guide or hear how it's said, that's okay!

To ensure that you're still using your phrases, you can review more than 1-5 phrases at a time on a schedule that works for your family.

THE LONG-TERM GAME

Again, the child's vocabulary should increase steadily, say, at the rate of half a dozen words a day. Think of fifteen hundred words in a year! The child who has that number of words, and knows how to apply them, can speak French." - *Charlotte Mason*[8]

After using this guide, if you would like to continue using a language with your family while making exponetial progress, I would love to invite you to the full TalkBox.Mom program!

TalkBox.Mom is the only immersion program of its kind that helps your entire family start talking the same day you start and guides you far down the path of fluency to where the language is a part of your everyday life.

As your family follows our proven roadmap with all the busy work done for you, you'll receive your core language guides already printed in a series of nine boxes. Each box dives deep into a specific area of your home life while offering various fluency approaches to help your family pass up years of trying to speak another language.

As you receive your printed guides at a pacing of your choice, your new box appears in the TalkBox.Mom Companion App, opening up to the native speaker audio for that box, additional resources, and a system to track your progress. As you reach the end of the boxes, your guides are almost exclusively in the language you're learning!

Most families order their first box with our phrasebook. The phrases found in this guide *Bilingual in Nature* are just a few phrases from each of our phrasebooks that have over 1,750 phrases.

If you'd like TalkBox.Mom to give you all the tools and support you need to start talking in another language with your family, get started in the language of your choice at **www.talkbox.mom/start.**

MY STORY

Before I read the words of Charlotte Mason and M. Gouin, I too realized that "the classical method, with its grammar, its dictionary, and its translations, is a delusion."[9]

You see, my husband and I put everything in storage to travel around the world with our two boys to play and explore outside. We started in Brazil, and I had a verb conjugation book, a college textbook, vocabulary cards, and two little boys to learn Portuguese with!

I had tried learning other languages this same way (well, minus the little boys)—only to leave me feeling anxious whenever I went to speak. But this is how learning a language is done, right? When I announced to my three-year-old that we needed to learn to conjugate a verb before going outside, he stared at me like I was out of my mind and said, "We didn't come to Brazil to sit in a room."

And I realized that he said this wise statement without ever learning to conjugate verbs or without ever looking at flashcards. As someone who studied philosophy and languages at the University, I was self-aware enough to realize that I had been sucked into a very flawed but widespread model of language learning. It hit me that parents teach languages so much faster and before their kids can read—without grammar and vocab worksheets.

So I decided that I was going to teach a language like a mom and learn like a child with my family. Within two weeks, I was shocked when we were talking in and understanding Portuguese with native speakers in Brazil. Absolutely shocked. And as the months rolled on, we kept talking and understanding more and more.

From country to country, I continued to develop and optimize this approach as we traveled for two years. Each time we learned faster and were reaching our goal: really speaking the language! Queue a whole ton of fireworks!

But this wasn't enough. I knew any family could learn a language this way. Not just mine. I could feel it in my heart. You specifically were in my heart. Your hopes, your dreams of being able to use another language with your family. Before I ever met you here, I was thinking about you and knew I needed to do this for you.

So I created TalkBox.Mom with an amazing team of women to give you life-changing results.

I know that when you and your family can actually use a language you can change your future work and educational opportunities. You can help others in your community. You can connect with family. You can make real connections as you travel. You can truly become a *global citizen*.

If you're not a TalkBox.Mom family yet, go to **www.talkbox.mom/start** and choose your language for your first box and book to get started. Then please introduce yourself in our private accountability group. You'll get a personal invitation to this group.

I'd love to know what led you to want to learn a language with your family and which language you chose.

I want to meet you! I want to hear your progress and see you reach your daily goals. Afterall, I made TalkBox.Mom for you.

See you there!

xo,
Adelaide

USE SPANISH IN NATURE

How To Guide on Page 7

Focusing on this phrase!

♥ ☑ *Using this phrase!*

		outside	afuera
♡ ☐		Do you want to go outside?	¿Quieres salir (afuera)?
♡ ☐		Do you want to play outside?	¿Quieres salir a jugar?
♡ ☐		Let's play outside.	Vamos a salir a jugar.

		to walk	caminar
♡ ☐		Let's go on a walk.	Vamos a caminar.

the path el camino

Follow the path.   Sigue el camino.

(to 2+)   Sigan el camino.

the puddle   el charco

Let's jump in the puddles.   Vamos a brincar en los charcos.

Look! **¡Mira!**

(to 2+) ¡Miren!

Look right there.   Mira ahí.

Look at the dog.   Mira el perro.

the poop   la popó

♡☐   Look out! Don't step in the poop.   ¡Cuidado! No pises la popó.

the river   el río

♡☐   The river is going very fast.   El río corre muy rápido.

♡☐   The river is going very slow.   El río corre muy despacio.

the tree   el árbol

♡☐   Do you want to climb the tree?   ¿Quieres subirte al árbol?

♡☐   Look how tall the tree is!   Mira qué alto está ese árbol.

the shade   la sombra

♡ ☐   Let's go in the shade.   Vamos a caminar en la sombra.

♡ ☐   Let's sit in the shade.   Vamos a sentarnos en la sombra.

the leaf   la hoja

♡ ☐   The leaves are falling from the trees.   Las hojas se caen de los árboles.

♡ ☐   Here is a leaf.   Aquí está una hoja.

♡ ☐   Pick up the leaf.   Levanta la hoja.

the stick   el palo

♡ ☐   What a cool stick!   ¡Qué palo tan padre!

the flower **la flor**

♡☐ Look at those beautiful flowers. Mira esas flores tan hermosas.

the rock **la piedra**

♡☐ What a cool rock! ¡Qué piedra tan interesante!

♡☐ I want to take this rock home. Quiero llevarme esta piedra a la casa.

the lake **el lago**

♡☐ The lake is so beautiful. El lago es hermoso.

♡☐ We're going swimming in the lake. Vamos a nadar en el lago.

the grass   el pasto

♡☐   Come sit on the grass.   Ven a sentarte en el pasto.

♡☐   *(to 2+)*   Vengan a sentarse en el pasto.

It's time to...   Es hora de...

♡☐   It's time to go home.   Es hora de irse a la casa.

Falling in love with Spanish?
All of these phrases come from our phrasebook Use Spanish at Home, which has 1,700+ phrases. Upgrade to the full TalkBox.Mom experience with our phrasebook and boxes to use Spanish throughout your family's day. See page 16.

USE FRENCH IN NATURE

How To Guide on Page 7

Focusing on this phrase!

♥ ☑ *Using this phrase!*

outside   dehors

♡ ☐ Do you want to go outside?   Tu veux aller dehors ?

♡ ☐ Do you want to play outside?   Tu veux jouer dehors ?

♡ ☐ Let's play outside.   Viens, on va jouer dehors.
(Come on, we're going to play outside.)

♡ ☐ *(to 2+)*   Venez, on va jouer dehors.

to walk   marcher

♡ ☐ Let's go on a walk.   Viens, on va faire une promenade.
(Come on, we're going on a walk.)

♡ ☐ *(to 2+)*   Venez, on va faire une promenade.

the path   le chemin

♡ ☐   Follow the path.   Suis le chemin.

♡ ☐   *(to 2+)*   Suivez le chemin.

the puddle   la flaque

♡ ☐   Let's jump in the puddles.   Si on sautait dans les flaques ?
(How about we jump in the puddles?)

♡ ☐   **Look!   Regarde !**

♡ ☐   ***(to 2+)*   Regardez !**

♡ ☐   Look right there.   Regarde là-bas.

♡ ☐   Look at the dog.   Regarde le chien.

the poop   le caca

♡☐   Look out! Don't step in the poop.   Attention ! Ne marche pas dans le caca.

the river   la rivière

♡☐   The river is going very fast. *(a lot of current)*   Il y a beaucoup de courant dans la rivière.

♡☐   The river is going very slow. *(not a lot of current)*   Il n'y a pas beaucoup de courant dans la rivière.

the tree   l'arbre

♡☐   Do you want to climb the tree?   Tu veux grimper dans l'arbre ?

♡☐   Look how tall the tree is!   Regarde comme l'arbre est grand !

the shade — l'ombre

♡☐ Let's go in the shade. (*Come on, we're going to go in the shade.*) — Viens, on va se mettre à l'ombre.

♡☐ (*to 2+*) — Venez, on va se mettre à l'ombre.

♡☐ Let's sit in the shade. (*Come on, we're sitting to sit in the shade.*) — Viens, on va s'asseoir à l'ombre.

♡☐ (*to 2+*) — Venez, on va s'asseoir à l'ombre.

the leaf — la feuille

♡☐ The leaves are falling from the trees. — Les feuilles tombent des arbres.

♡☐ Here is a leaf. — Voici une feuille.

♡☐ Pick up the leaf. — Ramasse la feuille.

the stick — le bâton

♡☐ What a cool stick! — Trop cool le bâton !

♡☐ (*also*) — Trop chouette le bâton !

the flower **la fleur**

♡☐ Look at those beautiful flowers. Regarde ces jolies fleurs.

the rock **la pierre**

the pebble **le caillou**

♡☐ What a cool rock! Trop cool comme pierre !

♡☐ I want to take this rock home. Je veux ramener cette pierre à la maison.

the lake **le lac**

♡☐ The lake is so beautiful. Le lac est tellement beau !

♡☐ We're going swimming in the lake. On va nager dans le lac.

the grass *(in a field)*	**l'herbe**	
(on a lawn)	**la pelouse**	
(on a lawn) *(also)*	**le gazon**	
♡☐	Come sit on the grass.	Viens t'asseoir dans l'herbe.
♡☐	*(to 2+)*	Venez vous asseoir dans l'herbe.

It's time to...	**C'est l'heure de...**	
♡☐	It's time to go home.	C'est l'heure de rentrer à la maison.

Falling in love with French?

All of these phrases come from our phrasebook Use French at Home, which has 1,700+ phrases. Upgrade to the full TalkBox.Mom experience with our phrasebook and boxes to use French throughout your family's day. See page 16.

USE GERMAN IN NATURE

Focusing on this phrase!

How To Guide on Page 7

♥ ☑ *Using this phrase!*

	outside	**draußen**
♡ ☐	Do you want to go outside?	Möchtest du rausgehen?
♡ ☐	Do you want to play outside?	Möchtest du draußen spielen?
♡ ☐	Let's play outside.	Komm, wir gehen draußen spielen.
♡ ☐	*(to 2+)*	Kommt, wir gehen draußen spielen.

	to walk	**laufen**
♡ ☐	Let's go on a walk.	Lass uns spazieren gehen.
♡ ☐	*(to 2+)*	Lasst uns spazieren gehen.

the path   der Weg

Follow the path.   Folg dem Weg.

(to 2+)   Folgt dem Weg.

the puddle   die Pfütze

Let's jump in the puddles.   Komm, wir springen in die Pfützen.

(to 2+)   Kommt, wir springen in die Pfützen.

Look!   Schau mal!

(to 2+)   Schaut mal!

Look right there.   Schau mal, da drüben.

Look at the dog.   Schau mal, der Hund.

the poop *(to babies and toddlers)* **das Aa**

(to teenagers and grown ups) **die Kacke**

♡☐ Look out! Don't step in the poop. Pass auf! Tritt nicht in das Aa.

♡☐ *(to teenagers and grown ups)* Pass auf! Tritt nicht in die Kacke.

the river   der Fluss

♡☐ The river is going very fast. Der Fluss fließt sehr schnell.

♡☐ The river is going very slow. Der Fluss fließt sehr langsam.

the tree   der Baum

♡☐ Do you want to climb the tree? Möchtest du auf den Baum klettern?

♡☐ Look how tall the tree is! Schau mal, wie groß der Baum ist!

the shade   der Schatten

♡☐ Let's go in the shade. Komm, wir gehen (lieber) in den Schatten.

♡☐ *(to 2+)* Kommt, wir gehen (lieber) in den Schatten.

♡☐ Let's sit in the shade. Komm, wir setzen uns in den Schatten.

♡☐ *(to 2+)* Kommt, wir setzen uns in den Schatten.

the leaf   das Blatt

♡☐ The leaves are falling from the trees. Die Blätter fallen von den Bäumen.

♡☐ Here is a leaf. Hier ist ein Blatt.

♡☐ Pick up the leaf. Heb das Blatt auf.

the stick   der Stock

♡☐ What a cool stick! Was für ein cooler Stock!

the flower die Blume

♡☐ Look at those beautiful flowers. Schau dir diese schönen Blumen an.

the rock der Stein

♡☐ What a cool rock! Was für ein cooler Stein!

♡☐ I want to take this rock home. Ich möchte diesen Stein mit nach Hause nehmen.

the lake der See

♡☐ The lake is so beautiful. Der See ist wunderschön.

♡☐ We're going swimming in the lake. Wir gehen im See schwimmen.

the grass (*in a meadow*) **die Wiese**

the grass (*on a lawn*) **das Gras**

♡ ☐ Come sit on the grass. Komm, wir setzen uns auf die Wiese.

♡ ☐ (*to 2+*) Kommt, wir setzen uns auf die Wiese.

It's time to... Es ist Zeit...

♡ ☐ It's time to go home. Es ist Zeit, nach Hause zu gehen.

Falling in love with German?

All of these phrases come from our phrasebook Use German at Home, which has 1,700+ phrases. Upgrade to the full TalkBox.Mom experience with our phrasebook and boxes to use German throughout your family's day. See page 16.

USE ITALIAN IN NATURE

Focusing on this phrase!

How To Guide on Page 7

♥☑ *Using this phrase!*

	outside	**fuori**
♡☐	Do you want to go outside?	Vuoi andare fuori?
♡☐	Do you want to play outside?	Vuoi giocare fuori?
♡☐	Let's play outside.	Andiamo a giocare fuori.

	to walk	**camminare**
♡☐	Let's go on a walk.	Andiamo a fare una passeggiata.

the path   il sentiero

♡☐   Follow the path.   Segui il sentiero.

♡☐   *(to 2+)*   Seguite il sentiero.

the puddle   la pozzanghera

♡☐   Let's jump in the puddles.   Saltiamo nelle pozzanghere.

♡☐   **Look!   Guarda**!

♡☐   *(to 2+)*   **Guardate!**

♡☐   Look right there.   Guarda là.

♡☐   Look at the dog.   Guarda il cane.

the poop   la cacca

♡☐   Look out! Don't step in the poop.   Attenzione! Non calpestare la cacca.

the river   il fiume

♡☐   The river is going very fast.   Il fiume scorre molto veloce.

♡☐   The river is going very slow.   Il fiume scorre molto lento.

the tree   l'albero

♡☐   Do you want to climb the tree?   Vuoi arrampicarti sull'albero?

♡☐   Look how tall the tree is!   Guarda com'è alto l'albero!

the shade **l'ombra**

♡☐   Let's go in the shade.   Andiamo all'ombra.

♡☐   Let's sit in the shade.   Sediamoci all'ombra.

the leaf **la foglia**

♡☐   The leaves are falling from the trees.   Le foglie stanno cadendo dagli alberi.

♡☐   Here is a leaf.   Ecco una foglia.

♡☐   Pick up the leaf.   Raccogli la foglia.

the stick **il bastone**

♡☐   What a cool stick!   Bello quel bastone!

the flower   il fiore

♡☐   Look at those beautiful flowers.   Guarda che bei fiori.

the rock   il sasso

♡☐   What a cool rock!   Che bel sasso!

♡☐   I want to take this rock home.   Voglio portare a casa questo sasso.

the lake   il lago

♡☐   The lake is so beautiful.   Il lago è davvero bello.

♡☐   We're going swimming in the lake.   Stiamo andando a nuotare al lago.

the grass (*in a field / country side*)   **l'erba**

♡☐   Come sit on the grass.   Vieni a sederti sull'erba.

♡☐   (*to 2+*)   Venite a sedervi sull'erba.

It's time to...   È ora di...

♡☐   It's time to go home.   È ora di andare a casa.

Falling in love with Italian?
All of these phrases come from our phrasebook Use Italian at Home, which has 1,700+ phrases. Upgrade to the full TalkBox.Mom experience with our phrasebook and boxes to use Italian throughout your family's day. See page 16.

USE CHINESE {MANDARIN} IN NATURE

Focusing on this phrase!

How To Guide on Page 7

♥ ☑ *Using this phrase!*

	outside	外面
		wài miàn
♡ ☐	Do you want to go outside?	你想去外面吗?
		nǐ xiǎng qù wài miàn ma?
♡ ☐	(to 2+)	你们想去外面吗?
		nǐ men xiǎng qù wài miàn ma?
♡ ☐	Do you want to play outside?	你想去外面玩吗?
		nǐ xiǎng qù wài miàn wán ma?
♡ ☐	(to 2+)	你们想去外面玩吗?
		nǐ men xiǎng qù wài miàn wán ma?
♡ ☐	Let's play outside.	让我们去外面玩。
		ràng wǒ men qù wài miàn wán.

Chinese is a Tonal Language

In the Pinyin (phonetics), you'll notice marks above some of the vowels. These are the tones the vowels make. If there is no mark, the tone is neutral. Words written with the same vowel can be different words based on their tone. Have fun listening to and mimicking the tones!

steady high	medium to high	low, lower, high	high to low
ā ē ī ō ū ǖ	á é í ó ú ǘ	ǎ ě ǐ ǒ ǔ ǚ	à è ì ò ù ǜ

to walk 散步
sàn bù

to walk 走
zǒu

♡□ Let's go on a walk. 我们去散个步吧。
wǒ men qù sàn ge bù ba.

the path 小路
xiǎo lù

♡□ Follow the path. 沿着小路。
(to one or 2+) yán zhe xiǎo lù.

TALKBOX.MOM

the puddle 水坑
shuǐ kēng

♡☐ Let's jump in the puddles. 让我们一起在水坑里跳吧。
ràng wǒ men yì qǐ zài shuǐ kēng lǐ tiào ba.

♡☐ **Look!** 看!
kàn!

♡☐ Look at the dog. 看那条狗。
kàn nà tiáo gǒu.

♡☐ Look right there. 看那里。
kàn nà lǐ.

the poop 屎
shǐ

♡☐ Look out! Don't step in the 小心! 不要踩到屎。
poop. xiǎo xīn! bú yào cǎi dào shǐ.

the river *(small river)* 河
hé

the river *(large river)* 江
jiāng

♡☐ The river is going very fast. 河流得非常快。
hé liú de fēi cháng kuài.

♡☐ The river is going very slow. 河流得非常慢。
hé liú de fēi cháng màn.

the tree 树
shù

♡☐ Do you want to climb the tree? 你想要爬树吗?
nǐ xiǎng yào pá shù ma?

♡☐ *(to 2+)* 你们想要爬树吗?
nǐ men xiǎng yào pá shù ma?

♡☐ Look how tall the tree is! 看这棵树多么高啊!
kàn zhè kē shù duō me gāo a!

the shade 阴凉处
yīn liáng chù

♡ ☐ Let's go in the shade. 我们去阴凉处吧。
wǒ men qù yīn liáng chù ba.

♡ ☐ Let's sit in the shade. 我们坐在阴凉处吧。
wǒ men zuò zài yīn liáng chù ba.

the leaf 树叶
shù yè

♡ ☐ The leaves are falling from 树叶正从树上落下来。
the trees. shù yè zhèng cóng shù shàng luò xià lái.

♡ ☐ Here is a leaf. 这有一片树叶。
zhè yǒu yí piàn shù yè.

♡ ☐ Pick up the leaf. 捡起树叶。
jiǎn qǐ shù yè.

the stick 棍子
gùn zi

♡ ☐ What a cool stick! 多么特别的棍子呀!
duō me tè bié de gùn zi ya!

the flower 花
huā

♡ ☐ Look at those beautiful flowers. 看那些漂亮的花。
kàn nà xiē piào liàng de huā.

the rock (*rock*) 石头
shí tou

(*boulder*) 岩石
yán shí

♡ ☐ What a cool rock! 多么特别的石头呀!
duō me tè bié de shí tou ya!

♡ ☐ I want to take this rock home. 我想把这块石头带回家。
wǒ xiǎng bǎ zhè kuài shí tou dài huí jiā.

the lake　湖
hú

♡ ☐ 　The lake is so beautiful.　湖是那样美丽。
hú shì nà yàng měi lì.

♡ ☐ 　We're going swimming in
the lake.　我们要去湖里游泳。
wǒ men yào qù hú lǐ yóu yǒng.

the grass　草
cǎo

(in a field / countryside)　草地
cǎo dì

(on a lawn)　草坪
cǎo píng

♡ ☐ 　Come sit on the grass.　过来坐在草地上。
(to one or 2+)　guò lái zuò zài cǎo dì shàng.

It's time to... 该••••••了
(to one or 2+) gāi—le

♡□ It's time to go home. 该回家了。
gāi huí jiā le.

Falling in love with Chinese?

All of these phrases come from our phrasebook Use Chinese
{Mandarin} at Home, which has 1,700+ phrases. Upgrade to the
full TalkBox.Mom experience with our phrasebook and boxes to
use Mandarin throughout your family's day. See page 16.

USE JAPANESE IN NATURE

Focusing on this phrase!

How To Guide on Page 7

♥ ☑ *Using this phrase!*

	outside	外 soto
♡ ☐	Do you want to go outside?	お外に行きたい？ Osotoni ikitai?
♡ ☐	Do you want to play outside? (*Won't you play outside?*)	外で遊ばない？ Sotode asobanai?
♡ ☐	Do you want to play outside? (*less pushy*)	外で遊びたい？ Sotode asobitai?
♡ ☐	Let's play outside!	外で遊ぼう！ Sotode asobou!

to walk **散歩**
sanpo

♡ □   Let's go on a walk.   お散歩に行こう。
Osanponi ikou.

the path **道**
michi

♡ □   Follow the path.   道に沿っていって。
Michini sotte itte.

the puddle **水たまり**
mizutamari

♡ □   Let's jump in the puddles.   水たまりの中でジャンプしちゃおう。
Mizutamarino nakade janpu shichaou.

♡ ☐   **Look!**   **見て!**
Mite!

♡ ☐   Look at the dog.   **あの犬見て。**
Ano inu mite.

♡ ☐   Look right there.   **そこ見て。**
Soko mite.

the poop   **うんち**
unchi

♡ ☐ Look out! Don't step in the poop.   **気をつけて!うんち踏んじゃダメだよ。**
Kiwo tsukete! Unchi funja damedayo.

Is it okay to speak Japanese before reading Japanese?

Yes! In fact, it's better for your pronunciation, promotes fluency, and will help you read Japanese faster.

Charlotte Mason taught that "the child should never see [foreign language] words in print until he has learned to say them with as much ease and readiness as if they were English."[10]

Note, as a reference and reminder between listening to the audio, we provide the transliteration (the phrase written in the English alphabet) to aid you.

the river 川
kawa

♡☐ The river is going very fast.
(*The flow of the river is fast.*)
川の流れがすごく速いよ。
Kawano nagarega sugoku hayaiyo.

♡☐ The river is going very slow.
(*The flow of the river is slow.*)
川の流れがすごくゆっくりだよ。
Kawano nagarega sugoku yukkuri dayo.

the tree 木
Ki

♡☐ Do you want to climb the tree?
木登りしたい？
Kinobori shitai?

♡☐ Look how tall the tree is!
見て！すごく高い木だよ！
Mite! Sugoku takai ki dayo!

the shade 日陰
hikage

♡☐   Let's go in the shade.   日陰に行こう。
Hikageni ikou.

♡☐   Let's sit in the shade.   日陰に座ろう。
Hikageni suwarou.

the leaf 葉
ha

♡☐   The leaves are falling from the trees.   木から葉っぱが落ちてるね。
Kikara happaga ochiterune.

♡☐   Here is a leaf.   はい、葉っぱ。
Hai, happa.

♡☐   Pick up the leaf.   葉っぱ、拾って。
Happa hirotte.

the stick 棒
bou

♡☐   What a cool stick!   わあ！かっこいい棒！
Waa! Kakkoii bou!

the flower 花
hana

♡☐ Look at those beautiful flowers. あの綺麗なお花見て。
Ano kireina ohana mite.

the rock 石
ishi

the pebble 小石
koishi

♡☐ What a cool rock! わあ、かっこいい石!
Waa, kakkoii ishi!

♡☐ I want to take this rock home. この石、お家に持って帰りたい。
Kono ishi, ouchini motte kaeritai.

the lake　湖
mizuumi

♡☐　The lake is so beautiful.　湖、すごく綺麗だね。
Mizuumi sugoku kireidane.

♡☐　We're going swimming in　湖で泳ぐよ。
the lake.　Mizuumide oyoguyo.

the grass (*in a field*)　草
kusa

(*on a lawn*)　芝生
shibafu

♡☐　Come sit on the grass.　こっちの草の上に座ろうよ。
Kocchino kusano ueni suwarouyo.

It's time to... **...する時間だよ。**
...suru jikandayo.

♡□   It's time to go home.   家に帰る時間だよ。
Ieni kaeru jikandayo.

Falling in love with Japanese?

All of these phrases come from our phrasebook Use Japanese at
Home, which has 1,700+ phrases. Upgrade to the full
TalkBox.Mom experience with our phrasebook and boxes to use
Japanese throughout your family's day. See page 16.

USE KOREAN IN NATURE

How To Guide on Page 7

Focusing on this phrase!

❤☑ *Using this phrase!*

	outside	밖
		bak

❤☐ Do you want to go outside?
밖에 나가고 싶어?
bak-ggeh nah-gah-goh seep-eo?

❤☐ *(honorific)*
밖에 나가고 싶어요?
bak-ggeh nah-gah-goh seep-eo-yo?

❤☐ Do you want to play outside?
밖에 나가서 놀고 싶어?
bak-ggeh nah-gah-seo nol-goh seep-eo?

❤☐ *(honorific)*
밖에 나가서 놀고 싶어요?
bak-ggeh nah-gah-seo nol-goh seep-eo-yo?

❤☐ Let's play outside.
(우리) 밖에서 놀자.
(woo-lee) bak-ggeh-seo nol-jah.

❤☐ *(honorific)*
(우리) 밖에서 놀아요.
(woo-lee) bak-ggeh-seo nol-ah-yo.

When to Use Honorific Expressions

In Korean, honorific expressions are used in the home:

(1) if a pre-teen child or older child is speaking to a parent,

(2) if a child of any age or an adult is speaking to a grandparent,

(3) sometimes for older generations, if a younger spouse is speaking to an older spouse that is about five years or older, and

(4) if a parent is teaching a toddler to use honorific expressions.

You can choose to start with only honorific expressions as you begin, and later, when you're comfortable with your phrases, learn to use the other set of phrases.

	to walk	**걷다** **geot-dah**
♡ ☐	Let's go on a walk.	(우리) 산책하자. (woo-lee) san-chaek-hah-jah.
♡ ☐	*(honorific)*	(우리) 산책해요. (woo-lee) san-chaek-hae-yo.

What are titles?

In Korean, some honorific expressions, like in the phrase, "Do you want to climb a tree?" require you to use the person's name or title. In the TalkBox.Mom Companion App, we have a list of titles for you to choose from. These include titles like, mom, younger sibling, cousin, or grandma.

	the path	길
		geel

♡□ Follow the path. 길 따라가.
geel ddah-lah-gah.

♡□ *(honorific)* 길 따라가세요.
geel ddah-lah-gah-seh-yo.

	the puddle	웅덩이
		woong-deong-ee

♡□ Let's jump in the puddles. 웅덩이 안으로 점프하자.
woong-deong-ee an-eu-loh jeom-peu-
hah-jah.

♡□ *(honorific)* 웅덩이 안으로 점프해요.
woong-deong-ee an-eu-loh jeom-peu-
hae-yo.

♡ ☐   Look!   **저것 봐 봐!**
                             jeo-geot bwah bwah!

♡ ☐   *(honorific)*   **저것 보세요!**
                             jeo-geot boh-seh-yo!

♡ ☐   Look at the dog.   저 강아지 봐 봐.
                             jeo gang-ah-jee bwah bwah.

♡ ☐   *(honorific)*   저 강아지 보세요.
                             jeo gang-ah-jee boh-seh-yo.

♡ ☐   Look right there.   바로 저길 봐.
                             bah-loh jeo-geel bwah.

♡ ☐   *(honorific)*   바로 저길 보세요.
                             bah-loh jeo-geel boh-seh-yo.

               the poop   **똥**
                             ddong

       (to a baby)   **응가**
                             eung-gah

♡ ☐ Look out! Don't step in the   조심해! 똥 밟지 마.
                   poop.   joh-seem-hae! ddong bal-jee mah.

♡ ☐   *(honorific)*   조심하세요! 똥 밟지 마세요.
                             joh-seem-hah-seh-yo! ddong bal-jee
                             mah-seh-yo.

the river 강
gang

♡☐ The river is going very fast. 강이 너무 빨리 흘러가.
gang-ee neo-moo bbal-lee heul-leo-gah.

♡☐ *(honorific)* 강이 너무 빨리 흘러가요.
gang-ee neo-moo bbal-lee heul-leo-gah-yo.

♡☐ The river is going very slow. 강이 천천히 흘러가.
gang-ee cheon-cheon-hee heul-leo-gah.

♡☐ *(honorific)* 강이 천천히 흘러가요.
gang-ee cheon-cheon-hee heul-leo-gah-yo.

the tree 나무
nah-moo

♡☐ Do you want to climb the tree? 나무 올라가고 싶어?
nah-moo ol-lah-gah-goh seep-eo?

♡☐   *(honorific)* *(name or title)* 나무 올라가고 싶어요?
                              (name or title) nah-moo ol-lah-gah-goh seep-eo-yo?

♡☐   Look how tall the tree is!   저 나무 큰 것 봐봐!
                              jeo nah-moo keun geot bwah-bwah!

♡☐   *(honorific)*   저 나무 큰 것 보세요!
                              jeo nah-moo keun geot boh-seh-yo!

the shade   **그늘**
                   geu-neul

♡☐   Let's go in the shade.   (우리) 그늘로 들어가자.
                              (woo-lee) geu-neul-loh deul-eo-gah-jah.

♡☐   *(honorific)*   (우리) 그늘로 들어가요.
                              (woo-lee) geu-neul-loh deul-eo-gah-yo.

♡☐   Let's sit in the shade.   (우리) 그늘에 앉자.
                              (woo-lee) geu-neul-eh an-jah.

♡☐   *(honorific)*   (우리) 그늘에 앉아요.
                              (woo-lee) geu-neul-eh an-jah-yo.

the leaf **잎**
eep

(also) **나뭇잎**
nah-moot-neep

♡☐ The leaves are falling from the trees. 나무에서 잎이 떨어진다.
nah-moo-eh-seo eep-ee ddeol-eo-jeen-dah.

♡☐ *(honorific)* 나무에서 잎이 떨어져요.
nah-moo-eh-seo eep-ee ddeol-eo-jyeo-yo.

♡☐ Here is a leaf. 여기 나뭇잎 있어.
yeo-gee nah-moot-neep iss-eo.

♡☐ *(honorific)* 여기 나뭇잎 있어요.
yeo-gee nah-moot-neep iss-eo-yo.

♡☐ Pick up the leaf. 나뭇잎 주워.
nah-moot-neep joo-weo.

♡☐ *(honorific)* 나뭇잎 주우세요.
nah-moot-neep joo-woo-seh-yo.

the stick **막대기**
mak-dae-gee

♡☐ What a cool stick! 멋진 막대기다!
meot-jeen mak-dae-gee-dah!

♡☐ *(honorific)* 멋진 막대기예요!
meot-jeen mak-dae-gee-yeh-yo!

the flower 꽃
ggot

♡☐ Look at those beautiful flowers. 저기 꽃 이쁜 것 봐봐.
jeo-gee ggot ee-bbeun geot bwah-bwah.

♡☐ *(honorific)* 저기 꽃 이쁜 것 보세요.
jeo-gee ggot ee-bbeun geot boh-seh-yo.

the rock 돌
dol

♡☐ What a cool rock! 돌이 멋있다!
dol-ee meo-seet-dah!

♡☐ *(honorific)* 돌이 멋있네요!
dol-ee meo-seet-neh-yo!

♡☐ I want to take this rock home. 이 돌 집에 가져가고 싶어.
ee dol jeeb-eh gah-jyeo-gah-goh seep-eo.

♡☐ *(honorific)* 이 돌 집에 가져가고 싶어요.
ee dol jeeb-eh gah-jyeo-gah-goh seep-eo-yo.

the lake **호수**
hoh-soo

♡ ☐ The lake is so beautiful. 호수가 너무 이쁘다.
hoh-soo-gah neo-moo ee-bbeu-dah.

♡ ☐ *(honorific)* 호수가 너무 이뻐요.
hoh-soo-gah neo-moo ee-bbeo-yo.

♡ ☐ We're going swimming in (우리) 호수에서 수영할 거야.
the lake. (woo-lee) hoh-soo-eh-seo soo-yeong-hal geo-yah.

♡ ☐ *(honorific)* (우리) 호수에서 수영할 거예요.
(woo-lee) hoh-soo-eh-seo soo-yeong-hal geo-yeh-yo.

the grass **풀밭**
(in a field/countryside) **pool-bat**

(on a lawn) **잔디밭**
jan-dee-bat

♡ ☐ Come sit on the grass. 와서 풀밭에 앉아.
wah-seo pool-bat-eh an-jah.

♡ ☐ *(honorific)* 와서 풀밭에 앉아요.
wah-seo pool-bat-eh an-jah-yo.

It's time to... **... 시간이야.**

... see-gan-ee-yah.

♡☐ It's time to go home. 집에 갈 시간이야.

jeeb-eh gal see-gan-ee-yah.

♡☐ *(honorific)* 집에 갈 시간이에요.

jeeb-eh gal see-gan-ee-eh-yo.

Falling in love with Korean?

All of these phrases come from our phrasebook Use Korean at Home, which has 1,700+ phrases. Upgrade to the full TalkBox.Mom experience with our phrasebook and boxes to use Korean throughout your family's day. See page 16.

USE BRAZILIAN PORTUGUESE IN NATURE

Focusing on this phrase!

How To Guide on Page 7

♥ ☑ *Using this phrase!*

	outside	fora
♡ ☐	Do you want to go outside?	Você quer ir lá fora?
♡ ☐	Do you want to play outside?	Você quer brincar lá fora?
♡ ☐	Let's play outside.	Vamos brincar lá fora.
♡ ☐	*(informal)*	A gente vai brincar lá fora.

	to walk	andar
	(to go on a walk)	caminhar
♡ ☐	Let's go on a walk.	Vamos andar.
♡ ☐	*(informal)*	A gente vai andar.
♡ ☐	*(also)*	Vamos caminhar.
♡ ☐	*(also) (informal)*	A gente vai caminhar.

the path   o caminho

Follow the path.   Segue o caminho.

(to 2+)   Sigam o caminho.

the puddle   a poça

Let's jump in the puddles.   Vamos pular nas poças.

(informal)   A gente vai pular nas poças.

Look!   Olha!

(to 2+)   **Olhem!**

Look at the dog.   Olha o cachorro.

Look right there.   Olha lá.

the poop   o cocô

♡☐   Look out! Don't step in the poop.   Cuidado! Não pisa no cocô.

the river   o rio

♡☐   The river is going very fast.   O rio está muito rápido.

♡☐   The river is going very slow.   O rio está muito devagar.

the tree   a árvore

♡☐   Do you want to climb the tree?   Você quer subir na árvore?

♡☐   Look how tall the tree is!   Olha como a árvore é alta!

the shade   a sombra

♡☐   Let's go in the shade.   Vamos pra sombra.

♡☐   *(informal)*   A gente vai pra sombra.

♡☐   Let's sit in the shade.   Vamos sentar na sombra.

♡☐   *(informal)*   A gente vai sentar na sombra.

the leaf   a folha

♡☐   The leaves are falling from the trees.   As folhas estão caindo das árvores.

♡☐   Here is a leaf.   Aqui uma folha.

♡☐   Pick up the leaf.   Pega a folha.

the stick   o graveto

♡☐   What a cool stick!   Que graveto legal!

the flower **a flor**

♡☐ Look at those beautiful flowers. Olha aquelas flores lindas.

the rock **a pedra**

♡☐ What a cool rock! Que pedra legal!
♡☐ I want to take this rock home. Quero levar essa pedra pra casa.

the lake **o lago**

♡☐ The lake is so beautiful. O lago é tão lindo
♡☐ We're going swimming in the lake. Vamos nadar no lago.
♡☐ *(informal)* A gente vai nadar no lago.

the grass   a grama

♡☐ Come sit on the grass.   Vem sentar na grama.

♡☐ (*to 2+*)   Venham sentar na grama.

It's time to…   Está na hora de…

♡☐ It's time to go home.   Está da hora de ir pra casa.

Falling in love with Portuguese?
All of these phrases come from our phrasebook Use Portuguese at Home, which has 1,700+ phrases. Upgrade to the full TalkBox.Mom experience with our phrasebook and boxes to use Portuguese throughout your family's day. See page 16.

USE HEBREW IN NATURE

How To Guide on Page 7

Focusing on this phrase!

♥ ☑ *Using this phrase!*

	outside	בחוץ
		bah'utz

♥ ☐	Do you want to go outside? (to a male)	רוצה לצאת החוצה?
		rotze latzet hah'utza?
♥ ☐	(to a female)	רוצה לצאת החוצה?
		rotza latzet hah'utza?
♥ ☐	(to a male)	רוצה לשחק בחוץ?
		rotze lesah'ek bah'utz?
♥ ☐	(to a female)	רוצה לשחק בחוץ?
		rotza lesah'ek bah'utz?
♥ ☐	Let's play outside? (to a male)	בוא נשחק בחוץ?
		bo nesah'ek bah'utz?
♥ ☐	(to a female)	בואי נשחק בחוץ?
		boi nesah'ek bah'utz?

♡ ☐ Let's play outside! **בוא נשחק בחוץ!**
(*to a male*) bo nesah'ek bah'utz!

♡ ☐ (*to a female*) **בואי נשחק בחוץ!**
boi nesah'ek bah'utz!

♡ ☐ (*to 2+*) **בואו נשחק בחוץ!**
bou nesah'ek bah'utz!

to walk **ללכת**
laleh'et

♡ ☐ Let's go on a walk. **בוא נלך לטייל.**
(*to a male*) bo neleh' letayel.

♡ ☐ (*to a female*) **בואי נלך לטייל.**
boi neleh' letayel.

♡ ☐ (*to 2+*) **בואו נלך לטייל.**
bou neleh' letayel.

the path **השביל**
hashvil

♡ ☐ Follow the path. **תעקוב אחר השביל.**
(*to a male*) ta'akov ah'ar hashvil.

♡ ☐ (*to a female*) **תעקבי אחר השביל.**
ta'akvi ah'ar hashvil.

♡ ☐ (*to 2+*) **תעקבו אחר השביל.**
ta'akvu ah'ar hashvil.

Native Speaker Audio – Page 4 –

the puddle	**השלולית**	
	hashlulit	

♡☐ Let's jump in the puddles. *(to a male)* **בוא נקפוץ בשלוליות.** bo nikfotz bashluliyot.

♡☐ *(to a female)* **בואי נקפוץ בשלוליות.** boi nikfotz bashluliyot.

♡☐ *(to 2+)* **בואו נקפוץ בשלוליות.** bou nikfotz bashluliyot.

♡☐ Look! *(to a male)* **תסתכל!** tistakel!

♡☐ *(to a female)* **תסתכלי!** tistakli!

♡☐ *(to 2+)* **תסתכלו!** tistaklu!

♡☐ Look right there. *(to a male)* **תסתכל לשם.** tistakel lesham.

♡☐ *(to a female)* **תסתכלי לשם.** tistakli lesham.

♡☐ Look at the dog. *(to a male)* **תסתכל על הכלב.** tistakel al hakelev.

(to a female) תסתכלי על הכלב.
tistakli al hakelev.

הקקי **the poop**
hakaki

Look out! Don't step in the תיזהר! אל תדרוך על הקקי.
poop. (to a male) tizaher! al tidroh' al hakaki.

(to a female) תיזהרי! אל תדרכי על הקקי.
tizahari! al tidreh'i al hakaki.

הנהר **the river**
hanahar

The river is going very fast. הנהר זורם מהר מאוד.
hanahar zorem maher meod.

The river is going very הנהר זורם לאט מאוד.
slow. hanahar zorem leat meod.

העץ the tree
haetz

♡☐ Do you want to climb the tree? (*to a male*) **רוצה לטפס על העץ?**
rotze letapes al haetz?

♡☐ (*to a female*) **רוצה לטפס על העץ?**
rotza letapes al haetz?

♡☐ Look how tall the tree is! (*to a male*) **תראה כמה גבוה העץ!**
tir'e kama gavoha haetz!

♡☐ (*to a female*) **תראי כמה גבוה העץ!**
tir'i kama gavoha haetz!

הצל the shade
hatzel

♡☐ Let's go in the shade. (*to a male*) **בוא נלך בצל.**
bo neleh' batzel.

♡☐ (*to a female*) **בואי נלך בצל.**
boi neleh' batzel.

♡☐ (*to 2+*) **בואו נלך בצל.**
bou neleh' batzel.

♡☐ Let's sit in the shade. בוא נשב בצל.
(*to a male*) bo neshev batzel.

♡☐ (*to a female*) בואי נשב בצל.
boi neshev batzel.

♡☐ (*to 2+*) בואו נשב בצל.
bou neshev batzel.

העלה the leaf
ha'ale

♡☐ The leaves are falling from העלים נושרים מן העצים.
the trees. ha'alim noshrim min haeytzim.

♡☐ Here is a leaf. הינה עלה.
hine ale.

♡☐ Pick up the leaf. (*to a male*) תרים את העלה.
tarim et ha'ale.

♡☐ (*to a female*) תרימי את העלה.
tarimi et ha'ale.

המקל the stick
hamakel

♡☐ What a cool stick! איזה מקל מגניב!
eyze makel magniv!

the flower **הפרח**
haperah'

♡☐ Look at those beautiful תסתכל על הפרחים היפים האלה.
flowers. (*to a male*) tistakel al haprah'im hayafim haele.

♡☐ (*to a female*) תסתכלי על הפרחים היפים האלה.
tistakli al haprah'im hayafim haele.

the rock **האבן**
haeven

♡☐ What a cool rock! איזו אבן מגניבה!
eyzo even magniva!

♡☐ I want to take this rock אני רוצה לקחת את האבן הזאת הביתה.
home. (*for a male*) ani rotze lakah'at et haeven hazot
habayta.

♡☐ (*for a female*) אני רוצה לקחת את האבן הזאת הביתה.
ani rotza lakah'at et haeven hazot
habayta.

the lake **האגם**
ha'agam

♡☐ The lake is so beautiful. האגם כל כך יפה.
ha'agam kol kah' yafe.

♡☐ We're going swimming in אנחנו הולכים לשחות באגם.
the lake. (*for a male*) anah'nu holh'im lis'h'ot ba'agam.

♡☐ (*for a female*) אנחנו הולכות לשחות באגם.
anah'nu holh'ot lis'h'ot ba'agam.

the grass **הדשא**
hadeshe

♡☐ Come sit on the grass. בוא שב על הדשא.
(*to a male*) bo shev al hadeshe.

♡☐ (*to a female*) בואי שבי על הדשא.
boi shvi al hadeshe.

♡☐ (*to 2+*) בואו שבו על הדשא.
bou shvu al hadeshe.

It's time to...　　**הגיע הזמן ל...**
　　　　　　　　　hegia hazman le/la...

♡☐　It's time to go home.　　הגיע הזמן לללכת הביתה.
　　　　　　　　　　　　　hegia hazman laleh'et habaita.

Falling in love with Hebrew?

All of these phrases come from our phrasebook Use Hebrew at Home, which has 1,700+ phrases. Upgrade to the full TalkBox.Mom experience with our phrasebook and boxes to use Hebrew throughout your family's day. See page 16.

In Hebrew, certain phrases are said differently based on the gender of the speaker and/or the gender of the person or people receiving the message.

Next to every phrase like this, there is a note that says *(to a male)*, *(to a female)*, *(for a male)*, and *(for a female)*.

(to a male) and *(to a female)* mean that the phrase is being said to a male or a female respectively.

(for a male) and *(for a female)* mean that the phrase is for a male to say or for a female to say respectively.

If a phrase does not have a note, the phrase can be said to or by any gender.

The note *(to 2+)* that you see in Hebrew and other languages notes a phrase that is specifically said to two people or more.

USE RUSSIAN IN NATURE

Focusing on this phrase!

How To Guide on Page 7

♥ ☑ *Using this phrase!*

	outside *(idiomatic: on the street)*	**на улице** **na ulitse**
♡ ☐	Do you want to go outside?	Хочешь на улицу? Hochesh na ulitsu?
♡ ☐	Do you want to play outside?	Хочешь поиграть на улице? Hochesh paigrat' na ulitse?
♡ ☐	Let's play outside.	Давай поиграем на улице. Davay paigrayem na ulitse.
♡ ☐	*(to 2+)*	Давайте поиграем на улице.Davayte paigrayem na ulitse.

to walk **ходить**
hadit'

♡ ☐ Let's go on a walk. Давай пойдём погуляем.
Davay paydyom pagulyayem.

♡ ☐ *(to 2+)* Давайте пойдём погуляем.
Davayte paydyom pagulyayem.

the path **дорожка**
darozhka

♡ ☐ Follow the path. Иди по дорожке.
Idi pa darozhke.

♡ ☐ *(to 2+)* Идите по дорожке.
Idite pa darozhke.

the puddle **лужа**
luzha

♡ ☐ Let's jump in the puddles. Давай прыгать по лужам.
Davay prygat` pa luzham.

♡ ☐ *(to 2+)* Давайте прыгать по лужам.
Davayte prygat` pa luzham.

♡☐ Look! **Смотри!**
Smatri!

♡☐ (to 2+) **Смотрите!**
Smatrite!

♡☐ Look at the dog. **Посмотри на собаку.**
Pasmatri na sabaku.

♡☐ Look right there. **Смотри туда.**
Smatri tuda.

the poop какашки
kakashki

♡☐ Look out! Don't step in the poop. **Осторожно! Не наступи на какашки.**
Astarozhna! Ne nastupi na kakashki.

the river река
reka

♡☐ The river is going very fast. **Река течёт очень быстро.**
Reka techyot ochen' bystra.

♡ ☐　The river is going very slow.　Река течёт очень медленно.
Reka techyot ochen' medlenna.

the tree　дерево
dereva

♡ ☐　Do you want to climb the tree?　Ты хочешь залезть на дерево?
Ty hochesh zalezt' na dereva?

♡ ☐　Look how tall the tree is!　Посмотри, какое высокое дерево!
Pasmatri, kakoye vysokaye dereva!

the shade　тень
ten'

♡ ☐　Let's go in the shade.　Пойдём в тень.
Paydyom v ten'.

♡ ☐　(to 2+)　Пойдёмте в тень.
Paydyomte v ten'.

♡ ☐　Let's sit in the shade.　Давай посидим в тени.
Davay pasidim v teni.

♡ ☐　(to 2+)　Давайте посидим в тени.
Davayte pasidim v teni.

the leaf **листок**
listok

♡☐ The leaves are falling from the trees. | Листья падают с деревьев.
List'ya padayut s derev'yev.

♡☐ Here is a leaf. | Вот листок.
Vot listok.

♡☐ Pick up the leaf. | Подними листок.
Padnimi listok.

the stick **палка**
palka

♡☐ What a cool stick! | Какая классная палка!
Kakaya klassnaya palka!

the flower **цветок**
tsvetok

♡☐ Look at those beautiful flowers. | Посмотри, какие красивые цветы.
Pasmatri, kakiye krasiviye tsvety.

the rock **камень**
kamen'

♡☐ What a cool rock! Какой классный камень!
Kakoy klassniy kamen'!

♡☐ I want to take this rock home. Я хочу взять этот камень домой.
Ya hachu vzyat' etat kamen' damoy.

the lake **озеро**
ozera

♡☐ The lake is so beautiful! Озеро такое красивое!
Ozera takoye krasivaye!

♡☐ We're going swimming in the lake. Мы идём купаться в озере.
My idyom kupatsa v ozere.

the grass **трава**
trava

♡ ☐   Come sit on the grass.   Садись на траву.
Sadis' na travu.

♡ ☐   *(to 2+)*   Садитесь на траву.
Sadites' na travu.

It's time to... **Пора...**
Para...

♡ ☐   It's time to go home.   Пора идти домой.
Para itti damoy.

Falling in love with Russian?

All of these phrases come from our phrasebook Use Russian at Home, which has 1,700+ phrases. Upgrade to the full TalkBox.Mom experience with our phrasebook and boxes to use Russian throughout your family's day. See page 16.

Reference List

1   Mason, Charlotte M. (1925). *Home Education*, 301.
2   Mason, Charlotte M. (1925). *Home Education*, 157.
3   Mason, Charlotte M. (1925). *Home Education*, 301.
4   Mason, Charlotte M. (1925). *Home Education*, 80.
5   Mason, Charlotte M. (1925). *Home Education*, 80.
6   Mason, Charlotte M. (1925). *Home Education*, 80.
7   Mason, Charlotte M. (1925). *Home Education*, 301.
8   Mason, Charlotte M. (1925). *Home Education*, 80.
9   Mason, Charlotte M. (1925). *Home Education*, 306.
10 Mason, Charlotte M. (1925). *Home Education*, 301.

TALKBOY MOM